discovermore

Learning Social Studies Skills

Exploring Secondary Sources

Marie Harts

Britannica Educational Publishing

IN ASSOCIATION WITH

THE ROSEN PUBLISHING GROUP

Published in 2025 by The Rosen Publishing Group, Inc.
2544 Clinton Street, Buffalo, NY 14224

Editor: Shannon Harts
Book Design: Michael Flynn

Photo Credits: Cover Nigita/Shutterstock.com; (series background) Dai Yim/Shutterstock.com; p. 4 Gary Perkin/Shutterstock.com; p. 5 Robyn of Exeter/Shutterstock.com; p. 7 (top) Everett Collection/Shutterstock.com; p. 7 (bottom) https://commons.wikimedia.org/wiki/File:Biographies_and_stories_of_Abraham_Lincoln_(1865)_(14742055826).jpg; p. 8 courtesy of the Library of Congress; p. 9 wavebreakmedia/Shutterstock.com; p. 10 Federico Rostagno/Shutterstock.com; p. 11 r.classen/Shutterstock.com; p. 12 IB Photography/Shutterstock.com; p. 13 NDAB Creativity/Shutterstock.com; p. 15 (top) monticello/Shutterstock.com; p. 15 (bottom) https://commons.wikimedia.org/wiki/File:Pulitzer_Prizes_(medal).png; p. 17 (top) DimaBerlin/Shutterstock.com; p. 17 (bottom) Vereshchagin Dmitry/Shutterstock.com; p. 18 Kaspars Grinvalds/Shutterstock.com; p. 19 yurii_yurii/Shutterstock.com; p. 20 Dean Drobot/Shutterstock.com; p. 21 Thapana_Studio/Shutterstock.com; p. 23 (top) isak55/Shutterstock.com; p. 23 (bottom) Feng Yu/Shutterstock.com; p. 24 OHishiapply/Shutterstock.com; p. 25 Pheelings media/Shutterstock.com; p. 26 Richard OD/Shutterstock.com; p. 27 Motortion Films/Shutterstock.com; p. 28 Sasun Bughdaryan/Shutterstock.com; p. 29 New Africa/Shutterstock.com.

Cataloging-in-Publication Data

Names: Harts, Marie.
Title: Exploring secondary sources / Marie Harts.
Description: New York : Britannica Educational Publishing, in Association with Rosen Educational Services, 2025. | Series: Discover more: learning social studies skills | Includes glossary and index.
Identifiers: ISBN 9781641901475 (library bound) | ISBN 9781641901468 (pbk) | ISBN 9781641901482 (ebook)
Subjects: LCSH: History--Research--Juvenile literature. | History--Sources--Juvenile literature. | Information resources--Juvenile literature.
Classification: LCC D5.5 H347 2025 | DDC 907.2--dc23

Manufactured in the United States of America

CPSIA Compliance Information: Batch #CSBRIT25. For further information contact Rosen Publishing at 1-800-237-9932.

Contents

Discovering Stories

Telling stories is universal. That means it is done or experienced by all people around the world, so there are a lot of exciting stories to learn about! With so much to know, where do you start? Peek online. Visit a library. Look in your classroom. All of these places have resources to help you find facts. Many of these resources are secondary sources.

Using primary and secondary sources can help historians gather clues to solve famous historical mysteries, such as if there was truly a King Arthur. Stories about King Arthur have been told for around 1,000 years!

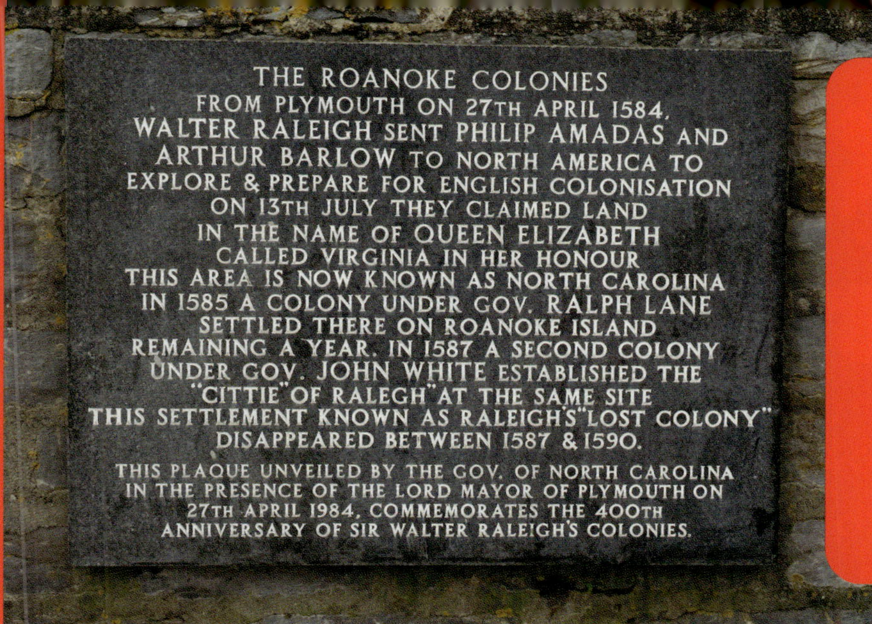

Another famous historical mystery is what happened to an English colony formed on Roanoke Island in 1587. Primary sources such as this historical marker and secondary sources, such as modern books about the colony, could help solve this mystery.

Both primary and secondary sources give information, or facts, about events, people, and places. A primary source is a work that gives original information. It is something that comes from the time being described or from a person who was involved in the events being described. A secondary source does not give original information. It explains information gathered from primary sources. Primary and secondary sources can help you understand stories from the past, and even act like a **detective** to solve mysteries of history!

WORD WISE

A DETECTIVE IS SOMEONE WHO WORKS TO FIND INFORMATION ABOUT SOMEONE OR SOMETHING.

Know the Questions to Ask

You may know it's important to ask questions when you want to find out information, but do you know what questions to ask? You should ask six questions when you want to learn new things: who, what, when, where, why, and how? The answers to these questions will help you to uncover clues and gather information.

Let's use a biography of Abraham Lincoln as a secondary source example. A biography is a story written about someone's life by someone other than who the book is about. Start by asking the six key questions. Who was Abraham Lincoln? What did Lincoln do? When did he live? Where did he live? Why was he important? How did he become president, or how did he make a difference? See how many of the questions you can answer. You may need another secondary source, such as a textbook, to answer some of the questions.

This photograph of Abraham Lincoln could be considered a primary source because it captures a moment in history.

compareandcontrast

How do you think the primary source of Abraham Lincoln's famous speech, the Gettysburg Address, can offer similar and different information from a secondary source, such as a book about the speech?

This biography about Abraham Lincoln was written long ago, around 1886, but it is still considered a secondary source because it offers an interpretation of Lincoln's life.

Searching School for Secondary Sources

Primary sources are often unique, or one of a kind, and can be hard to find. However, secondary sources might be all around you! Look for textbooks and other reference books that contain facts. Find history books to read about the past. Read maps to learn more about geography. Resources like these also are often published online.

This map is a primary source because it shows how the mapmaker understood the location of completed and planned telegraph lines in 1841. It would be a secondary source if it was a symbolic picture of a place.

While books can be great secondary sources for information, it's important to make sure they are reliable, or trustworthy. This can include making sure the author has credentials, or experience and education on the topic they are writing about.

Authors of secondary sources may use primary sources in their studies of a topic. An author of a biography could use an interview or a journal. Those are both primary sources. Photographs, drawings, maps, and letters made long ago also are primary sources. They help today's authors and illustrators to create history books and other secondary sources, such as posters. Your classroom and school are filled with resources like these! How many secondary sources can you find in one classroom, and what can they tell you about a topic?

Consider This

You can find both primary and secondary sources online too! Do you think it is easier to find primary or secondary sources online?

Discovering Sources at Home

School isn't the only place you can find primary and secondary sources—there might be many hiding at your home! Maybe someone in your family keeps a diary. Maybe your uncle writes poetry. These items are all primary sources, but you can find secondary sources at home too.

Magazine articles are often secondary sources because they interpret or comment on previous findings. But magazine articles can also be primary sources if they provide facts about a current event.

Newspaper articles, both print and online, are secondary sources if they provide a review or critique of past events. They are primary sources if they report on current events.

Maybe your home has magazines, books, or posters about the past. A poster about ancient Egypt that was made last year is an example of a secondary source. You know that the poster was not made during ancient Egyptian times. Therefore, it is not a primary source. In many homes, people read newspapers to learn about current and past events. Many newspaper articles are secondary sources. Today, newspaper articles are often published online. Some newspapers are only found online.

Consider This

Do you think a modern magazine article about 20th century women photographers would be a primary or a secondary source?

When Are Sources Reliable?

It can be exciting to find a primary or secondary source! It can also be useful if you are working on homework or another school project. However, before you use a primary or secondary source, it's important to know if it's reliable—especially if you found it on the internet.

Websites where you can find trustworthy secondary sources when researching often have URLs that end in either .org, .edu, or .gov.

Researching is studying to find something new. It is always important to make sure internet sources are trustworthy because on many websites, anyone can post anything!

When you use the internet to find information, use trustworthy websites. Websites that are reliable usually name an author or a group that has written the information. The author is often an **expert** in the subject. Reliable websites also tell the date the writing was posted. Don't use very old sites or sites with no author or editor names.

When you use a search engine, search for keywords instead of whole sentences. Keywords are the main ideas you want to know. Keywords of the sentence, "What are secondary sources about the Civil War?" are "secondary sources" and "Civil War."

WORD WISE

AN EXPERT IS A PERSON WITH SPECIAL SKILL IN OR KNOWLEDGE OF A SUBJECT.

Excellent Encyclopedias and More

A secondary source that is often considered reliable is an encyclopedia. It won't give you all the information on a topic. But it will give you general information to help you understand the important things about a topic. In an encyclopedia, authors give basic facts about topics. Encyclopedias used to be only printed in books. Today they are usually available online. You can use keywords to search for information on many different topics in an online encyclopedia.

Some excellent books receive awards. These books are good choices for learning. Bibliographies are lists of books and other resources about a topic. They may be a good place to begin learning too. Teachers, librarians, and media specialists can help you find reliable secondary sources like these. Media specialists are people who work at schools and help teachers and students with audiovisual tools, or tools that have audio and visual elements.

Wikipedia is a free online encyclopedia. While it can be reliable because it has an online community that makes sure articles have credible sources, it can also be unreliable because anyone can edit a Wikipedia page.

compareandcontrast

How do you think an online and print encyclopedia are similar and different? Do you think all online encyclopedias are trustworthy? Why or why not?

The Pulitzer Prize is an example of an award books can receive. Columbia University, in New York City, gives out a series of these awards to recognize major successes in American journalism, letters, and music.

Dependable Dewey Decimal System

United States public libraries have an average of about 116,482 items. With so many items, you may wonder how you can find the sources you are looking for! Libraries have special sorting systems to make it easier to find certain sources. When you know how they are grouped, you can find secondary sources more quickly.

Many libraries use a classification system called the Dewey Decimal System. In this system, nonfiction books are given a number, known as a call number. Call numbers are shown on each book's spine. The call number is based on the book's topic. In the Dewey Decimal System, topics are organized in 10 main groups of 100 numbers. For instance, all science and math books are in the 500 group.

While most public schools use the Dewey system, most academic libraries use another system called the Library of Congress Classification System (LC).

A library catalogue is a database that has a record for every item in a library, including all books, videos, sound recordings, and e-books. Today, catalogues are often digital, or found on a computer.

compare and contrast

In what ways do you think using a card system for a library catalogue is similar and different to a computerized system? What are some advantages of using either the computerized or card system?

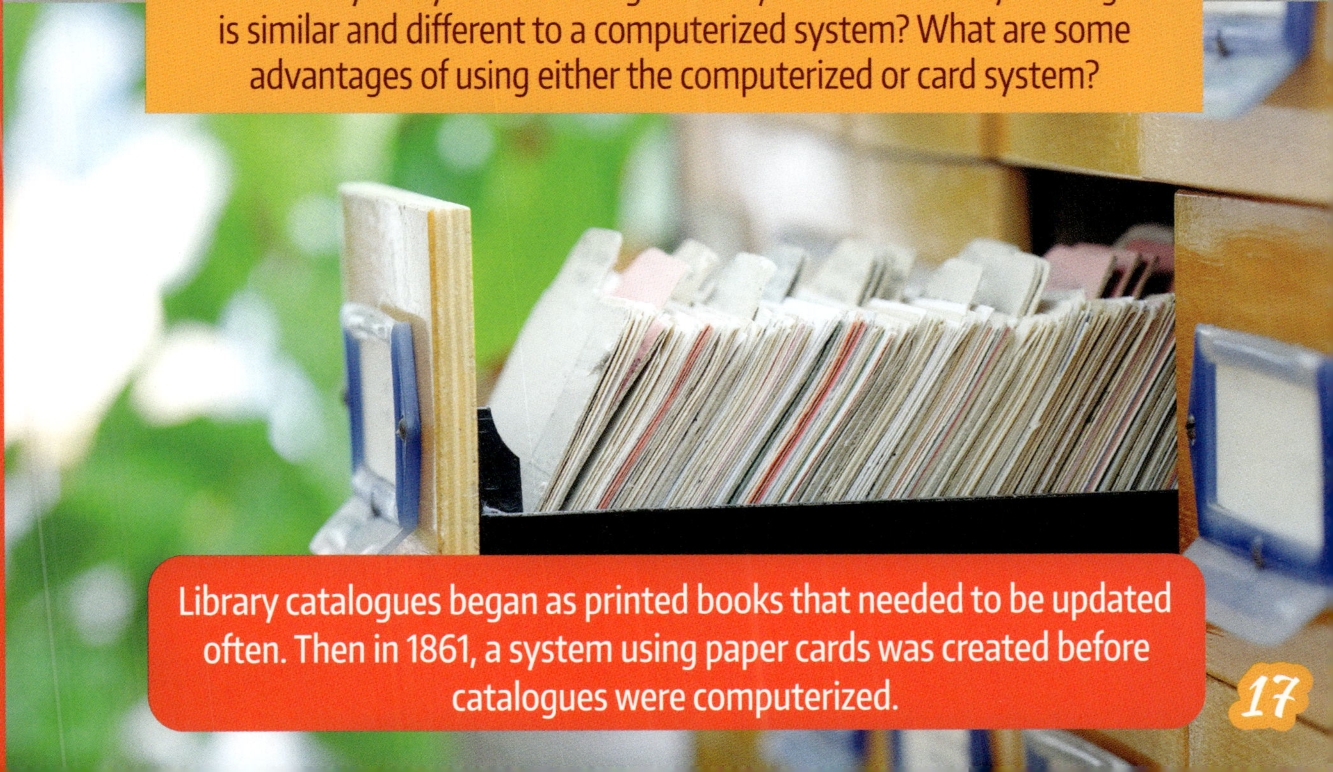

Library catalogues began as printed books that needed to be updated often. Then in 1861, a system using paper cards was created before catalogues were computerized.

Facts About Fake Sources

Today you can easily access a huge amount of information. Smartphones and laptops allow you to answer questions with a quick Google search. Many people also find information in articles shared on social media.

While it can be fun to watch videos on the popular social media app TikTok, it's important to know that misleading and even fake news videos have been found on the app.

Misleading and fake information has also been found on the social media app Facebook, which has almost 3 million monthly active users.

Unfortunately, some articles are unreliable. Some are fake, or completely made up. One way to make sure the news you read is true is to stick to well-known news groups. Another good idea is to look for the story elsewhere. If you can't find it, it might not be real. Also, check the article for all the important facts. Look for "who, what, when, and where" answers. Finally, look carefully at the title of the article. If the headline seems too wild to be true, it might be fake news. Fake news is often spread on social media. It's important to carefully check any article or other online source before you share it with others!

Consider This

People are more likely to believe and share fake news if it confirms a view or opinion they have. What are some views or opinions you have? Have you ever seen a fake news article that confirms these views?

The Difference Between Opinions and Facts

When you are researching a topic, you will likely find both facts and opinions. A fact can be proven. It states things that are real or that really happened. Opinions are things that people believe or feel to be true. Opinion pieces can be secondary sources if they explore an event, but they aren't as reliable as facts.

When trying to recognize if a source is more fact or opinion-based, it can help to consider why the source was created. Some different reasons include informing and educating, entertaining, or **persuading**.

Many believe the internet has made it harder to tell if information is based on facts or opinions. This is because information online is not always labeled with terms such as "Editorial" or "Op-Ed" that shows it's opinion based.

Not everything you read is a fact. When people try to convince you to believe something, they may use a mix of facts and opinions. Opinions often have words that describe how a person feels about something—for example, "good," "worst," and so on. Not all people would agree with those feelings. Facts, however, are not based on feelings or beliefs. Facts can be supported by evidence and can be used to create or inform an argument.

WORD WISE

TO PERSUADE IS TO CAUSE SOMEONE TO BELIEVE SOMETHING, OR TO CAUSE SOMEONE TO TAKE A CERTAIN ACTION BY ARGUING, GIVING REASONS, OR ASKING.

Start Learning with Secondary Sources!

There are many reasons to start your research with secondary sources. For example, secondary sources are often created to be easier for modern-day readers to understand.

Imagine if you had to learn from original documents only. To learn about George Washington, you might have to read his diary and letters! Searching for those primary sources could take a long time. Even if you found them, they might be very hard to read.

With secondary sources, you can get lots of information that is easier to find and understand. Secondary sources often have an index and a table of contents. These pages are helpful places to begin your quest for information. They can help you answer more specific research questions by finding just the right information.

An index is an alphabetical-order list of topics found in a book. Each index term includes page numbers to show where the topics can be found. An index is often found at the end of a book.

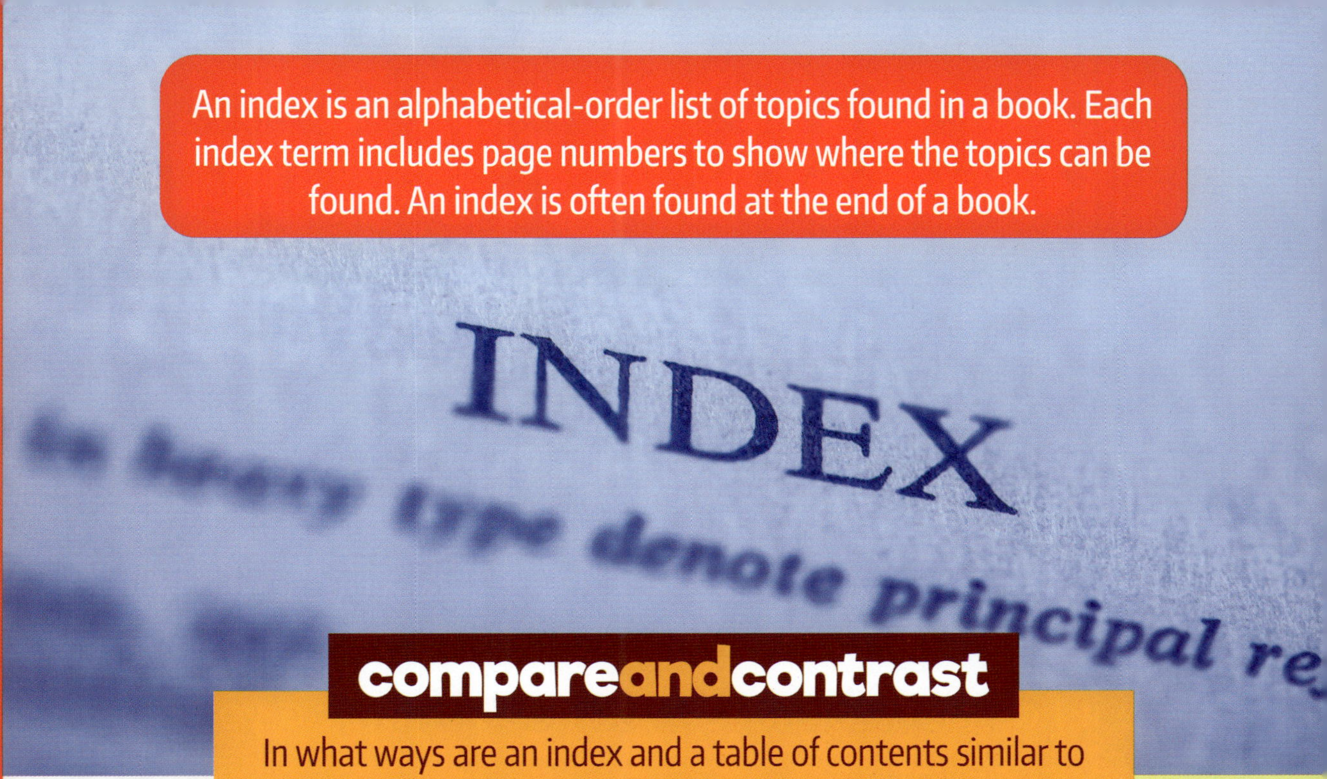

compare and contrast

In what ways are an index and a table of contents similar to and different from each other? Which do you think can be more helpful when trying to answer a research question?

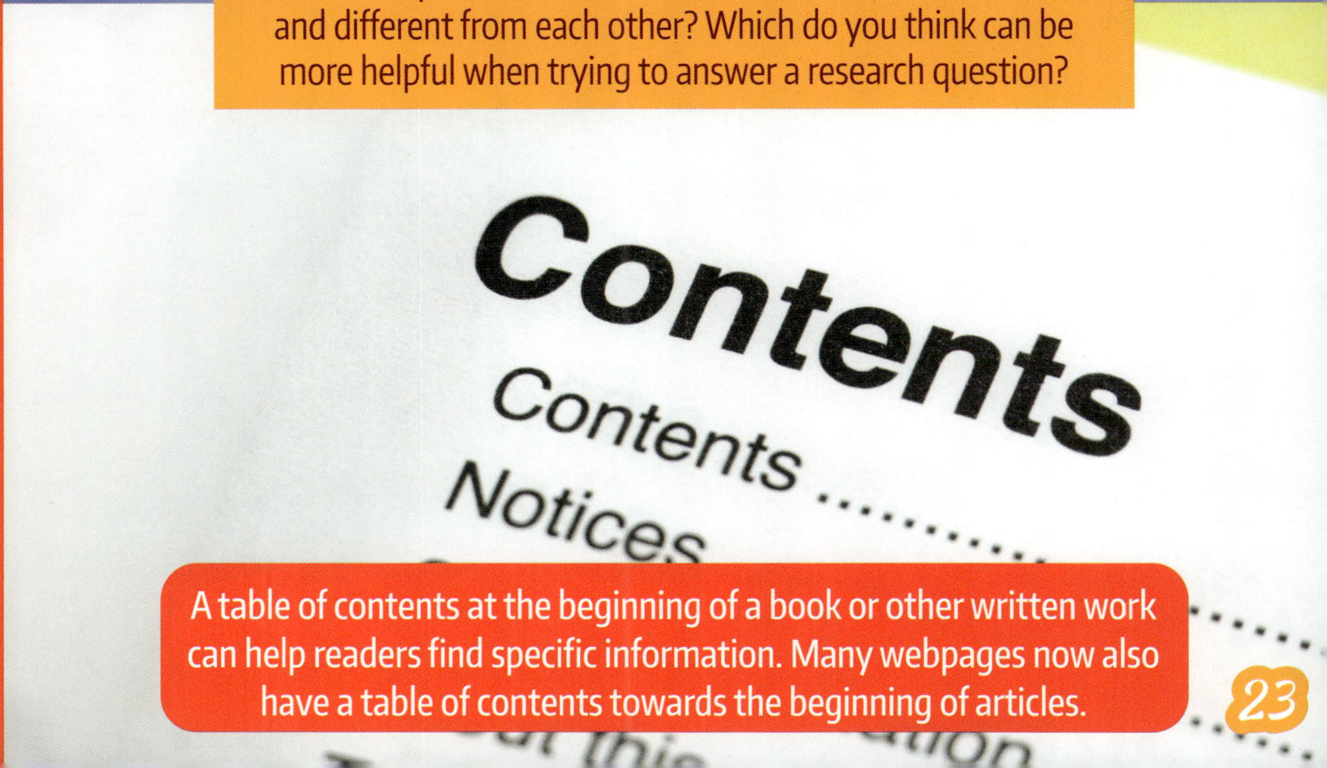

A table of contents at the beginning of a book or other written work can help readers find specific information. Many webpages now also have a table of contents towards the beginning of articles.

Skillfully Using Secondary Sources

While it's important to know how to find secondary sources, it is just as worthwhile to know the best ways to use secondary sources. Imagine that you have found what seems like the perfect resource. How can you be sure it has the information you need? How do you get the most out of it?

When creating summaries, it is often better to paraphrase **quotations** rather than copying every word of them. This means putting the meaning of the quotation in your own words.

Highlighting can help you understand and summarize what you have read, if you do it correctly. Some highlighting tips include only highlighting after you finish reading a section of text, and only highlighting key words.

Use everything in the source to help you. Preview the contents. Notice the headings and the topics in the index. Hunt for bold words, pictures, charts, maps, and other clues about main ideas. When you start reading, ask the "who, what, when, where, how, and why" questions. Summarizing is an important skill to practice while you learn new things. When you find something interesting, don't copy every word you read—unless you are copying a direct quotation. When summarizing, you instead state main ideas and only the most important facts to support those ideas.

WORD WISE

A QUOTATION IS SOMETHING THAT SOMEONE HAS SAID OR WRITTEN THAT SOMEONE ELSE REPEATS IN ANOTHER PIECE OF SPEECH OR WRITING. IT IS ENCLOSED IN QUOTATION MARKS (").

Your fingers can help you determine if a secondary source's reading level is just right for you. Read one page of a book or part of a website. While you read, hold up a finger for each word you don't know. At the end of that page or section, if you have up three or fewer fingers, the source is probably a good fit for you. If you have raised more than three fingers, you may need help reading the source. You may want to choose another source.

A glossary is a list that gives definitions of words that are unusual or a higher reading level.

If you prefer to type your notes about a source on a computer, some note-taking tips include grouping sources by publication type (such as grouping notes about books and websites together) and including URLs next to notes about websites.

Even as you read a "just right" resource, you might see new words. Use a glossary or dictionary to help you learn them. Before making any notes about a reading, think about the purpose behind your reading. After you write down facts and information that relate to this purpose, think about how they might connect to what you already know.

Consider This

When taking notes using index cards, it's suggested to use only one side of the cards, and to create a heading on each card. Why do you think these tips might be helpful?

Don't Be a Plagiarism Pirate!

While many people act like detectives when working on research projects, some act like pirates. Writing pirates steal words and ideas. They pretend those words are their own. Stealing ideas in this way is called plagiarism.

Plagiarism can lead to legal action if it goes against an author's copyright or **trademark**.

What mystery of history might you want to solve using primary and secondary sources?

Suppose you find a helpful website. You can write notes about it, but do not copy exactly what the website says. Authors spend time carefully researching when they write. Stealing an author's hard work is wrong. Instead, use your own words to share the ideas you have learned. Summarizing can help you do that. Remember to give authors credit for their work. When you take notes, write down the name of the resource and its author. Many secondary sources include a bibliography. You can learn to write one too. With a bibliography, everyone can see your sources. A bibliography can also help other readers acting like detectives find sources to answer research questions.

WORD WISE

A TRADEMARK IS SOMETHING, SUCH AS A WORD, THAT IDENTIFIES A CERTAIN COMPANY'S PRODUCT. IT CAN ONLY BE USED BY ANOTHER PERSON OR COMPANY WITH PERMISSION.

Glossary

Civil War A war fought from 1861 to 1865 in the United States between the Union (the Northern states) and the Confederacy (the Southern states).

copyright The legal right to be the only one to reproduce, publish, and sell a book, recording, or something else for a time period.

critique When someone gives a careful judgement that includes comments about the good and bad parts of something.

dictionary A reference book that has words listed in alphabetical order. It gives each word's meaning, forms, pronunciations, and more.

geography An area of study involving the location of countries, cities, mountains, likes, rivers, and other natural and man-made features.

illustrate To decorate a book or story with pictures.

interpretation The action or result of explaining or understanding something.

photographer A person who takes pictures with a camera.

preview To view or show in advance.

resource A source of information or support for learning.

telegraph An old-fashioned way of sending messages long distances using wires and electric signals.

symbolic Representing or expressing a quality or idea in a way that doesn't use words.

URL The letters and symbols that make up a website's address.

For More Information

Books

Banks, Rosie. *My First Look at Primary Sources.* New York, NY: Gareth Stevens Publishing, 2022.

Machajewski, Sarah. *Analyzing Sources of Information About the U.S. Constitution.* New York, NY: PowerKids Press, 2019.

Spanier, Kristine. *Using Primary Sources: Digital Citizenship.* Minneapolis, MN: Jump! Inc., 2019.

Websites

History in a Bag, Primary/Secondary Sources, Pablo Picasso
www.pbs.org/video/history-in-a-bag-primarysecondary-sources-pablo-picasso-h-ypc8dw/
This website features a video that covers primary and secondary sources, in addition to some facts about Pablo Picasso!

Primary Source
kids.britannica.com/kids/article/primary-source/629043
Learn more about the difference between primary and secondary sources here.

Index